NORTH WEST COAST
FROM THE AIR

AN AERIAL JOURNEY FROM BLACKPOOL TO CARLISLE

Ronny Mitchell

HALSGROVE

First published in Great Britain in 2009

British Library Cataloguing-in-Publication Data
A CIP record for this title is available from the British Library

ISBN 978 1 84114 907 3

HALSGROVE
Halsgrove House,
Ryelands Industrial Estate,
Bagley Road, Wellington, Somerset TA21 9PZ
Tel: 01823 653777   Fax: 01823 216796
email: sales@halsgrove.com

Part of the Halsgrove group of companies
Information on all Halsgrove titles is available at: www.halsgrove.com

Printed and bound by Grafiche Flaminia, Italy

Introduction
NORTH WEST COAST FROM THE AIR

The history of the North West Coast is dominated by the two centuries beginning about 1750 when the deposits of coal and iron ore which were to both enrich and scar the landscape were being discovered and exploited. New towns were built where none existed before and small fishing villages became industrial towns. The story has been well documented, but for those curious to gain a quick impression of the extent of it, a glance at the network of disused railway lines shown on the Ordnance Survey maps as "course of old railway" is revealing. I have spent many hours looking for these and other abandoned industrial sites from the air but finding them now is not easy. When the end of heavy industry came in the 1960s, it came suddenly and not much of it survived the thorough demolition which followed.

Tourism was not slow to take the place of industry which had occupied so many attractive sites on this varied and beautiful coast. Regeneration grants were made available to transform old industrial harbours into marinas creating a new life for people who had been deprived so abruptly of their traditional livelihoods. The so-called 'sunset industries' made way for the leisure activities of the twenty first century. My photographs will endeavour to show the results of some of these changes.

In my book *Lakeland & Cumbria from the Air* I suggested that readers might like to imagine flying with me as passengers, the caption to each picture being a substitute for the verbal explanation they would receive in flight. I make the same suggestion this time. The photographs have been taken over perhaps fifteen years and even in that short time much has changed. For example, two photographs show Whitehaven harbour both before and after the millennium development grant was made. Another two show an open cast coal site shortly after it was started and after its final restoration. Some things however have lasted unchanged through the turmoil of those two centuries such as canals and bridges, notably the magnificent Lune aqueduct and some of the original harbour works. The estuaries which we will fly over were, before the industrial period, clean and full of wildlife. Now they enjoy greater national and international protection than at any other time in the past three hundred years and the likelihood of damaging development occurring again becomes, hopefully, more remote every day but one must remain on one's guard. Tourism has rescued the coast from its industrial past. Let us hope that it has a care for the future.

Our flight from Blackpool to Carlisle is a distance of about 170 miles. If we were to stay close to the coast without deviating to either side it would take less than two hours in a light aeroplane. But we are in no hurry and as there is much of interest a short distance inland we will make a few diversions to explore beyond what is strictly defined as 'coast'. I have chosen subjects which, I hope, show the great diversity of this remarkable coastline, both the scenery and the structures, the old and the new, the good and the less good. But above all, this is a personal choice based on what has attracted my interest in the scenes which have unfolded below me over the years.

Ronny Mitchell.

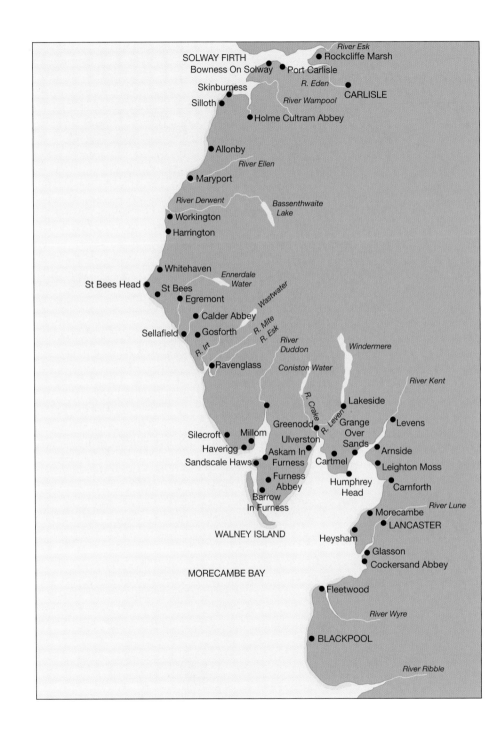

The design for Blackpool's most famous structure was inspired by the Eiffel Tower. It was first built in 1894 but after a fire on the platform and corrosion problems, it was rebuilt in 1924. Now, like the Forth Bridge, it is regularly repainted – a task that takes seven years. Being 518ft (160m) high and commanding an unrestricted view of the surrounding country, sea and skies it came in useful as a radar station during the war. It will be visible to us on our flight until we are on the far side of Black Combe on the coast of Cumbria.

Blackpool has three piers. North Pier is the earliest, intended for the quiet and more genteel leisure activities. This is Central Pier opened in 1868, intended more for fun with dancing, amusement arcades, bars and (since 1990) a ferris wheel 100ft (35m) high. The pier was ingeniously built on cast iron screw piles, driven down until reaching bedrock. Like most piers in Britain, this one suffered from fire, fortunately not catastrophic. When built, it was over 1500ft long (460m) which included a 400ft (120m) landing stage, later demolished.

Fleetwood scarcely existed before 1836 when a new town was planned by the architect Decimus Burton as a cheaper and more modest version of Blackpool. The result was an early Victorian planned town with streets laid out in a half wheel pattern. Burton also designed some of the fine buildings in the town such as the semi-circular North Euston Hotel (on the extreme right of the photograph) which he intended to be the rail terminus hotel for visitors from London. Another is the long building in the foreground which faced the railway station until that closed in 1966. He also designed the lighthouses to guide ships to the Wyre channel. The tallest, in broad Pharos Street, and another on the esplanade can be seen in the photograph. Along the river banks are the wharves for steamers and the Isle of Man passenger terminal.

Fleetwood's two main dock sections are the original Wyre Dock, completed in 1877, and beyond it the Fish Dock, completed in 1908 for the deep sea fishing fleet, then at the height of its prosperity. Now, since the drastic decline in fish stocks there are few deep water boats and the Fish Dock caters mainly for the diminished inshore fleet and for visiting boats to discharge their catch. This is processed in the sheds which surround the dock. There are plans to extend the Wyre Dock, now a marina, into half of the Fish Dock to create 150 new berths for leisure craft. There are also plans to develop the area around the dock to create Fleetwood Harbour Village. We will see more changes of this nature on our flight up the coast.

All that now remains of the Premonstratensian abbey of Cockersand, founded around 1200, is the Grade I listed polygonal chapter house which occupies its solitary bleak position at the mouth of the River Lune. Nothing else of the abbey's buildings is visible even from the air, usually the best vantage point for tracing the outlines of old foundations. At the Dissolution, monasteries became a valuable source of stone and this abbey was no exception. The chapter house survived because it was the burial place of the Daltons, a catholic family from Thurnham Hall. It is on private ground and therefore is not accessible to the public, although a public footpath runs close to the shore.

The chapter house has an entrance vestibule where it was attached to the east range of the cloister. We could surmise therefore that the nave, the cloister and other monastic buildings, built on the west (seaward) side of the chapter house, lay beyond what is now the shoreline. This implies that most would have been lost from coastal erosion had they not been deliberately demolished after the Dissolution in 1539.

Glasson Dock is situated on the final bend of the River Lune before it flows into Morecambe Bay. It was constructed in 1787 to be the port for Lancaster because even the small boats of the day were experiencing difficulty navigating the river up to the city. However, transhipment of cargoes was slow and expensive. So, some forty years later the Glasson arm, two and a half miles in length with six locks, was built to connect the dock to the Lancaster Canal which passed through the city centre. Glasson still has commercial traffic and the dock can handle ships up to 3000 tons. The old buildings in the photograph mostly date to the early nineteenth century.

Glasson marina occupies the Glasson Dock basin and at present has berths for 220 boats. But there are plans to extend this to create a total of 320 berths with some caravans and chalets. This view looks up the Glasson arm to its junction with the Lancaster Canal at Galgate. From 1883 to 1964, Glasson Dock had a railway connection whose trackbed can be seen starting on the seaward side of the dock basin and curving away to the left over the marshes to the bridge across the River Conder.

As we fly north, Heysham nuclear power station takes over from Blackpool Tower as the dominating feature of the skyline. There are in fact two power stations on the same site, each containing two advanced gas-cooled reactors. The nearer, Heysham 2, started generating in 1988 and the farther, Heysham 1 in 1983. Between them they can generate, it is said, enough electricity to keep six cities the size of Liverpool supplied at peak loading.

Heysham is one of Lancashire's three ports, all of which in their time have been important for the prosperity of the county. Two of them, Fleetwood and Glasson we have already looked at. Heysham, which was built in 1900, handles freight and daily passenger sailings to the Isle of Man.

Having the misfortune after nearly a thousand years to find a nuclear power station on one side and a brash holiday resort on the other, St Peter's Church still manages to retain its serenity and indifference to both. From its rocky promontory it has spectacular views across Morecambe Bay to the Furness fells. On its west side can be seen the ruins of eighth-century St Patrick's Chapel. Further west (closer to the camera) are the narrow slits of the famous rock-hewn 'graves', although these are more likely to be ossuaries or repositories of human bones because of their small size.

The western esplanade of Morecambe, formal gardens and white roof of the Morecambe Dome 'live entertainment venue' are on the left and in the left fore-ground is the refurbished Midland Hotel, a listed Grade II* art deco hotel built in 1933. Opposite the Hotel is the old railway station, both of which were built and operated by the London, Midland & Scottish Railway. The station is now an arts and information venue.

Prominent on their hilltop in the City of Lancaster are the Castle and the Priory Church of the Blessed Mary. The Priory Church was rebuilt, all but the tower, in the fifteenth century in the perpendicular style, and has glorious windows and choir stalls and a commanding position overlooking the city. The tower was rebuilt in the eighteenth century. Shortly after the Norman conquest the priory had become a cell of the Benedictine Abbey of St Martin of Seez in Normandy. When Henry V in 1414 suppressed all priories dependent upon foreign monasteries (the 'alien' priories) it was attached to the Brigittine convent of Syon in Middlesex, a mixed order uncommon in England. Thus it stayed until its dissolution in 1539. The castle has been a prison almost from the time of its foundation and it was here that the notorious trials of the Lancashire witches took place.

The Lancaster Canal crosses the River Lune on this magnificent aqueduct. It was designed by John Rennie and completed in 1796, its piers built on timber piles driven into the bed of the river. The mortar for the ashlar masonry was a mix of lime and pozzolana powder from Italy which enabled it to set under water. Rennie's profound and early knowledge of building techniques is well demonstrated by the way it has lasted.

Up to 1849 a daily water bus service crossed the aqueduct carrying passengers from Preston to Kendal with a journey time of just over seven hours. From here, the canal heads north through Hest Bank, Bolton le Sands, Carnforth to Tewitfield where it effectively ends. It was severed by the construction of the M6.

The rise and fall of Carnforth is typical of industry in the area. In 1800 Carnforth was little more than a village. The Lancaster Canal had just opened but it was not until the main line over Shap received parliamentary approval in 1844 that things began to change. The iron works began production of iron and later steel but it declined in the 1890s and closed in 1929. Carnforth was then a major junction of three railways whose large station had five platforms. By 1970 most of these had closed and been demolished but not before the classic film 'Brief Encounter' had ensured its claim to posterity. What you see in the photograph are the remains of the Motive Power Depot which maintained and supplied locomotives for the north-west railway system. Around 1969 it became Steamtown Museum which built up a collection of famous locomotives. Now sadly closed to the public it services steam engines in private ownership.

Silverdale is one station down the railway line to Barrow in Furness from Carnforth. It is then a short walk to Leighton Moss bird reserve which is owned and managed by the Royal Society for the Protection of Birds. It is the largest reedbed in north-west England, lies within the Arnside and Silverdale Area of Outstanding Natural Beauty and provides a habitat for reed buntings, bitterns, marsh harriers and many other species which may be viewed from the hides. There is also a visitor centre and cafeteria. This is the Moss in late winter, very conspicuous from the air in its glorious russet colours.

Above: Access to the marshes at Leighton Moss is via a track under the railway line to a small car park (beware of flooding when the tide is high!) The white track in the picture leads from the car park to a hide which can be seen on a neck of land between the first two lagoons.

Left: Leighton Moss in midsummer when all is once again lush and green.

North of Silverdale and within the Arnside and Silverdale Area of Outstanding Natural Beauty is the great scar of Middlebarrow Quarry visible for miles but now no longer worked. Its southern edge (left) stops just short of the boundary of Eaves Wood, an ancient oakwood owned by the National Trust. In the photograph we are looking over the wood to the Kent Estuary and Grange-over-Sands. On the extreme right of the wood can be seen Arnside Tower which is the subject of the next photograph.

Right: The second stop on the railway from Carnforth to Barrow in Furness on the old Furness Line is Arnside, a quiet seaside resort. Here the line crosses the Kent Viaduct, 600 yards (550m) long which was built by James Brunlees and opened in 1857. At the same time a branch from Arnside to Hincaster Junction on the main line to the north was opened. This can just be seen in the photograph, curving round the shore on the left from Arnside Station. It enabled the coke trains from Durham to reach the Furness iron works without having to reverse at Carnforth thus cutting eight miles from the route.

Opposite: On the edge of Middlebarrow wood is Arnside Tower, a pele tower of five storeys constructed in the fourteenth century in response to repeated Scots raids down the coast. Habitable to about 1680, it was then partly dismantled for building stone, which, together with storm damage, has left it in poor condition. Most pele towers were attached to domestic dwellings to provide instant refuge from raiders but Arnside Tower is freestanding.

The building of Levens Hall began with the construction of a pele tower in the thirteenth century after which many additions and alterations followed. The gardens were laid out by Guillaume Beaumont in the seventeenth century and contain remarkable topiary designs and formal bedding. Beaumont also planned the park on the opposite side of the A6. All is open to the public at specified times.

Like many of the great houses of Cumbria, Sizergh Castle started life as a pele tower in the fourteenth century for defence against the Scots raiders. It was much added to and altered in Elizabethan times and later and contains notable woodwork and furniture. Owned by the National Trust, the house and 14 acres (6 ha) of garden are open to the public.

Cumbria has two main areas of raised bogs. One is in the north of the county along the Solway Firth which we will be looking at later. The other is here between Levens and Grange-over-Sands. This photograph is of Foulshaw Moss, the largest single peat body in south Cumbria, until recently afforested with Scots pine and western hemlock, but still retaining its raised bog structure and rich in wild flowers and insects. In 1998 it was purchased by Cumbria Wildlife Trust who set about the task of restoration. They now manage it as a Site of Special Scientific Interest. The photograph shows Foulshaw six years after its purchase. The alien trees have gone, drainage channels have been blocked, the spread of rhododendron controlled and native oak woodland has been encouraged to return to the edges.

The next raised bog and a mile or two from Foulshaw is Meathop Moss, leased by Cumbria Wildlife Trust since 1963 and managed with the same objectives as Foulshaw. It has been a Nature Reserve since the 1920s and like Foulshaw is a Site of Special Scientific Interest. Most of the Trust's reserves are open to the public, but visitors should enquire before visiting. The photograph is looking north-east over Whitbarrow to the Lyth Valley.

Above: To the west of Grange-over-Sands is the spectacular carboniferous limestone spine of Humphrey Head reaching out into the Kent Estuary with impressive views across the waters of Morecambe Bay. It is 150ft (46m) high in the centre with cliffs on the near side and sloping grass on the far side. Its rich limestone flora merits its status as a Site of Special Scientific Interest, now managed by Cumbria Wildlife Trust. At its north end is based an outdoor education centre. Access is from a small car park at the northern end.

Opposite, far left: Holme Island was a true island until the causeway was built by the Brogden family in the nineteenth century. On either side of the causeway can be seen areas of spartina grass which is spreading in the estuary. The house which was built in the 1830s was occupied by the RAF during the war. In the woods near the tip of the island can be seen the dome of a reproduction Roman temple. Follies such as this were frequently built by wealthy landowners. The island is privately owned and there is no public access.

Opposite: Grange-over-Sands was a fishing village until the opening of the Kent Viaduct at Arnside in 1857 completed the coastal railway line around Cumbria from Carnforth to Carlisle. But it was traffic from the south which enabled Grange-over-Sands to grow as a seaside resort with large hotels and a promenade. The photograph looks over the town towards Holme Island and Arnside Knott.

We have already looked at two famous family homes, Levens Hall and Sizergh Castle. Holker Hall is another, the home of the Cavendish family. The first house was built in the sixteenth century and rebuilt in 1840 in a neo Elizabethan style. The west wing together with its valuable contents was destroyed by fire in 1871. Here we are looking at the Hall, its formal gardens and beyond to the park where the annual Holker garden festival is held. House and gardens are open to the public.

A short distance from Holker is the Augustinian Priory of Cartmel, founded in 1188 and dissolved by Henry VIII in 1536. But it was spared total destruction being the parish church as well as the church of the priory and the king did not wish to deprive his subjects of the right to worship. However, it suffered extensive damage and much of the church was left open to the weather for some sixty years until George Preston of Holker Hall undertook its restoration. The interior has a wonderful screen and choir stalls of the fifteenth century which, together with the large perpendicular east window, make it a chancel that must be unrivalled by any other parish church in the north. In the photograph we see the south side of the church with its unusual belfry set diagonally over the central tower.

At the dissolution of the priory in 1536, as well as substantial damage being done to the church itself, all but one of the domestic buildings were demolished, to be recycled as building material. The exception was the Gateway (in the photograph where the red van is parked) which was built in 1330-40 and housed the manorial court in the room above the archway, which no doubt was the reason for its survival. This is now in the care of the National Trust and is open to the public. Cartmel village is interesting and full of old houses and is of course famous for its sticky toffee pudding.

The Furness Line crosses the mouth of the Leven Estuary on a viaduct 500 yards long. It was built by the same engineer, James Brunlees, who in 1857 built the Kent Viaduct at Arnside. In the far distance, left, can be seen Humphrey Head.

Shortly after crossing the Leven Viaduct the railway comes to Plumpton Junction where a branch line went north to Lakeside at the southern end of Windermere. The line was opened in 1869 and enabled tourist trains from the midlands to connect with the lake steamers owned by the railway company. In the photograph is the village of Greenodd on the Leven Estuary. The railway crossed the Leven in the approximate position of the new footbridge.

This is the next bridge where the Lakeside line crossed the still tidal River Leven. In the background are the woods and raised bog of Roudsea National Nature Reserve. In September 1965 the line was closed from Plumpton Junction to Haverthwaite, but from 1973 it continued under the ownership of a preservation society to its terminus at Lakeside, operating a regular steam-hauled passenger service.

On the right is Lakeside where the line ended and passengers boarded the steamers. On the left is the National Trust's Fell Foot Park. Here, the River Leven leaves Windermere and passes Newby Bridge on its course to Haverthwaite and the estuary.

In a commanding position above Ulverston is Hoad Hill on the summit of which is the memorial built in 1850 to Sir John Barrow who was born in 1764. It is a copy of Smeaton's Eddystone lighthouse, an appropriate monument to one who was a founder member of the Royal Geographical Society, explorer, mathematician, author and eminent son of the town. It has been open to the public in the past but since 2003 has been closed.

The Ulverston Canal was constructed by the same engineer, John Rennie who built the Lune Aqueduct and in the same year, 1796. Ships up to 350 tons regularly passed through these locks and the canal itself being 300ft (91m) wide could act as a temporary harbour for boats awaiting tide or weather. The last ship to enter the canal was believed to have been in 1916. The stone jetty was used by the Liverpool Packet boats in 1835, now only by anglers.

This is the view up the Ulverston Canal from canal foot. The Glaxo works are on the left and the railway line crossing the canal two thirds of the way up is the old Plumpton Junction to Barrow line. This was started in 1883 but went no further than Conishead Priory when it was an expensive health hydro from 1878 to 1928. Note the canal locks at the bottom of the photograph.

This is the head of the Ulverston Canal and beyond it is the town centre. The cattle market is on the left of the basin and on the right is the curving terrace of houses named after Thomas Sunderland who was an early chairman of the canal company.

Chapel Island is a limestone outcrop a mile off shore near Conishead Priory. It has the ruins of an oratory built by the monks of Furness and was a staging post on the over-sands route from Cartmel to Ulverston which was made redundant when the railway opened in 1856. William Wordsworth in his poem 'The Prelude' described pausing there on his crossing of the sands.

Conishead Priory started as an Augustinian hospital in 1160, was elevated to priory status in 1188 and remained as such until its dissolution in 1537. It then went through a series of owners before becoming the home of the Bradyll family, the last of whom rebuilt the old house in the Gothic style. It is this fine house which is now Grade II* listed. It was a health hydro from 1878 to 1928 with its own railway connection to the main line. Further changes of ownership and use, including being a wartime hospital, occurred before it became the Manjushri Kadampa Meditation centre which then started a long and meticulous restoration. The photograph shows the huge extent of the Victorian Gothic house and also the newly completed Kadampa Buddhist temple.

On the outskirts of Ulverston is the outstanding Elizabethan Manor House, Swarthmoor Hall, which was built by George Fell in 1568. His son Judge Thomas Fell and his daughter in law Margaret invited George Fox, the itinerant Quaker preacher, to visit Swarthmoor Hall in 1652. This laid the foundations of the Religious Society of Friends who now own the house and run it as a Quaker retreat. It is open to the public at prescribed times.

The Woodland Trust owns over a thousand woods, but this one is unusual being an ancient semi natural woodland on boulder clay overlying limestone. Sea Wood therefore has varieties of trees and flora adapted to its soil and is a Site of Special Scientific Interest. There are records of oaks being felled in the wood and floated down to Ulverston for shipbuilding. The strip of shore beyond the road is a local Country Park.

South of Aldingham is Moat Farm. The moat at one time, perhaps in the early thirteenth century, may have been intended to provide protection from intruders such as smugglers. It is not open to the public.

Foulney Island was indeed once an island until the causeway along it was constructed in the nineteenth century to protect Walney Channel from silting up. The saltmarsh to the east has consequently developed a wide variety of vegetation. The island is composed of glacial pebbles brought from the Lake District by the last ice age and this provides the perfect breeding habitat for terns and other birds. Access therefore is not permitted during the breeding season when a warden occupies a caravan at the far end of the causeway. It is a Site of Special Scientific Interest leased and managed by Cumbria Wildlife Trust.

Fish traps laid out at low tide to the east of Foulney Island.

Roa Island, like Foulney was once a proper island with access only at low tide, but in 1846 a causeway was completed to extend the existing Furness Railway line which then terminated at Rampside. The 'thumb' of the island carried the railway to a pier which had three levels, on the upper of which was a station. Its length of 810ft (247m) enabled Fleetwood steamers to use the deep water of the channel at all states of the tide. The lifeboat station has recently been rebuilt and the small pier alongside is used by the ferry to Piel Island.

Piel Castle belonged to the monks of Furness Abbey. Its purpose is not precisely known but the existence of windows implies that it was not primarily military. It was more likely to have been a retreat for the abbot or for use as a safe place for documents or stores. It certainly enabled him to keep an eye on traffic in the channel in which the abbey had an interest. It is now in the care of English Heritage and can be visited by ferry from Roa Island.

Apart from the castle, Piel Island has only two other groups of houses. One is the 'Ship' Inn, down by the jetty on the left of the photograph, and the other a cluster of cottages believed to have been built for ships' pilots in the 1700s. The photograph is taken looking towards the southern tip of Walney Island.

This view of Piel Island is looking back towards Roa Island and shows the causeway which links the island to Rampside. William Wordsworth once spent a month at Rampside admiring the view across Piel Channel to the castle. In the distance is Barrow in Furness.

Walney Island lies to the west of Barrow in Furness and is linked to it by a road bridge constructed in 1908. This is the southern end, a sand and shingle bank which accommodates a nature reserve and the lighthouse at Hilpsford Point. The 'lakes' are left from old gravel workings. In the extreme lower left of the picture can be seen the burnt-out wharf where the gravel was loaded for shipment. Although there are good wild flowers the reserve is principally managed for birds and has a large mixed colony of black-backed and herring gulls. Access is by permit from the warden's house on entering the reserve.

Hilpsford Point lighthouse on the southern tip of Walney Island was constructed in 1790. The photograph shows it with the keepers' cottages in the foreground and stretching into the distance are Piel Island, Roa Island and to the right the shingle spit of Foulney Island.

Above: Here is *Artemis* docked in Ramsden Dock basin, Barrow, with other tall ships ready to welcome visitors.

Left: Periodically the 'tall ships' visit Cumbrian ports. This is *Artemis* cruising off Walney Island waiting for the tide to allow her to enter Piel Channel and Barrow Docks. *Artemis* is a 400 tonne barque built in 1926 and converted from freighter to luxury cruiser with a crew of 14 and berths for 35 passengers.

The old slipways are a reminder of Barrow's remarkable past. Here ships up to 103,000 tons have been constructed and launched into Walney Channel. From the 1850s the industry grew in importance and capability, building warships before the 1914 – 1918 war and reaching a peak in the immediate post war years. But from the 1960s it declined rapidly and the shipbuilding that now takes place is within the covered yards of British Aerospace's sheds built over Devonshire Dock.

Barrow's shipbuilding now takes place here in British Aerospace's covered shipyard built over Devonshire Dock. Beyond that is Buccleuch Dock leading into Ramsden Dock and in the far distance, Cavendish Dock, now a reservoir. Lower right is the east end of the bridge to Walney Island with its ornamental public garden.

Half way down Walney Island is Biggar Village which looks out over Piel Channel to Barrow Docks. Furness Abbey had a grange here in the thirteenth century and it is still a farming village with a pub. Walney Island has evidence of very early settlement; bronze age stone axes and arrow heads have been found and traces of medieval ridge and furrow cultivation can be seen at the southern end.

This view is looking up the west coast of Walney Island with the suburban spread of Vickerstown on the right. Walney Airfield which belongs to British Aerospace is beyond that and in the distance are the dunes of North Walney National Nature Reserve. The island is low lying with little shelter from the westerly winds but it nonetheless provided protection for Walney Channel and the shipyards.

The dunes of North Walney, Sandscale Haws and Haverigg are different from those further north as they are composed of lime rich sands and therefore have a more diverse flora. This is North Walney looking across Scarth Channel to Sandscale Haws. It is a National Nature Reserve well known and visited for its wild flowers and birds especially during migrations.

We are looking at low tide across the Duddon Estuary from North Walney towards Haverigg, Millom and Black Combe (2000ft or 610m). In the distance can be seen the wind turbines on the old wartime airfield at Millom.

The Duddon Estuary at low tide looking from North Walney reserve across Sandscale Haws to Askam in Furness and the snow covered fells of Central Lakeland. The estuary is recognised as being of such importance for wildlife that it has been designated a Special Protection Area under the European Birds Directive, a Special Area of Conservation under the European Habitats Directive, a Site of Special Scientific Interest under the Wildlife and Countryside Act of 1981 and a Ramsar wetland site of international importance.

The marram covered dunes of Sandscale Haws **a**re up to 100ft (30m) high with slacks between them which frequently fill with water in winter. This photograph was taken in early January and shows some of the flooded slacks. Sandscale is owned and managed by the National Trust and access is free at times when the dunes are not being grazed by cattle and sheep. In the distance is Askam in Furness and Ireleth with its small group of wind turbines.

We take a short diversion inland to look at Furness Abbey. When it was founded in 1124 the site the monks chose to settle in was an isolated sheltered valley 'far from the concourse of men'. It now lies close to the busy town of Barrow in Furness, a large hospital, a main road, a hotel and a railway line built in 1846 to the dismay of William Wordsworth. The first plan for the Furness Line took it through the Abbey's ruins and it was only to reduce the radius of the curve that it was re-routed through a tunnel thus enabling the line to skirt the edge of the abbey. Apart from founding many daughter houses, of which Calder Abbey is probably the best known, Furness had extensive properties as far away as Skelwith and was involved in every industry of the time. In the fourteenth century however Scots raids, famine and plague affected the abbey. Piel Castle was rebuilt in 1327 possibly as a garrison to protect and watch over the entrance to Piel harbour. Decline during the fifteenth century ended with dissolution in 1536. The photograph is taken looking south east towards the substantially intact building at the far end which is the chapel of the infirmary where old and sick monks were cared for. The Abbey is owned by English Heritage, is open to the public and has an excellent museum.

On our way back to the Duddon Estuary we pass Dalton. At the heart of this historic town is the castle, seen here in a well kept open public space. Originally it was a pele tower owned by Furness Abbey and used by them as a manorial court house. It later passed into the hands of the Duke of Buccleuch who gave it to the National Trust in 1965.

The town of Askam in Furness is close to, and just below, its older neighbour Ireleth. In the 1850s one of the richest deposits of iron ore in the country was discovered at Park Mine, Roanhead, close to Sandscale Haws (middle distance). Furnaces were constructed and were in full production from 1867 to their closure in 1918 followed by their demolition in 1933. Little trace now remains of an industry which was so crucial to the development of the Furness peninsula. In 1865 there was a proposal by the Furness Railway Company to construct a viaduct from Roanhead to Hodbarrow Point, but this came to nothing. At the same time the Whitehaven & Furness Junction Railway company proposed a crossing from Dunnerholme to Millom which also came to nothing.

The southern shore of Duddon Estuary is part of the Morecambe Bay European marine site and was until the 1960s a sprawling industrial region with all the pollution that that implies. Now it rests in relative peace, but a threat which has always been present has been the call to cross the mouth of the estuary with a bridge or a dam. In the caption to the previous picture of Askam I mentioned the two proposals made in 1865 to bridge the estuary. This is Dunnerholme which would have been the starting point for the more northerly crossing. It is a limestone outcrop on an otherwise sandy shore prominent from all parts of the estuary. There are lime kilns and good examples of ridge and furrow cultivation as seen here.

Another view of Dunnerholme from Kirkby-in-Furness with Askam and Sandscale Haws in the distance.

Industry has not all departed from the Duddon. The need for Kirkby quarry to transport its slate more easily than by boat from Kirkby Pool was an early reason for the construction of the Furness Railway. A map in the Cumbria Records Office, dated 1843, shows the proposal for a line from Kirkby to Rampside at Barrow with a branch to Lindal. This photograph shows the huge hole which is still worked for high quality slate, now transported by road. The original way of getting the slate to the slate works and the customer was down the incline (seen here) at first to barges in Kirkby Pool and later to the railway. The twelve wind turbines on Broughton Moor represent modern industry. The caravan site is typical of what creeps in to replace redundant industrial sites.

The river (lower left) is Kirkby Pool at Sandside where the original slate wharves were situated before the Furness Railway Company built the line which can be seen following the edge of the marsh past Dunnerholme and Askam.

Before we continue our flight along the north side of the estuary we will take a look at Duddon Furnace hidden in the coppiced woods which once provided much of its charcoal, now carpeted in spring with daffodils and other woodland flowers. Duddon Furnace was built in 1736 and continued smelting until 1867. The photograph shows the charcoal store (the farthest L-shaped building) built into the slope of the hill to enable carts to be unloaded directly into it. The roofed building was the iron ore store and the furnace with its charging platform is nearest. Water power for the blast furnace blowers was obtained from a weir half a mile up the river. Downstream beyond Duddon Bridge can still be seen the remains of the wharf used to bring ore to the site and to take away the iron. The whole furnace site has been carefully studied and restored by the National Park Authority and made accessible to the public.

The north side of Duddon Estuary is very different to the south. No dunes are evident here, only a great expanse of salt marsh, grazed by sheep. An earth bank which runs continuously from Foxfield to Millom protects the adjacent farmland from high tides.

Millom Castle is unusual in having a pele tower within its walls, whereas most peles are attached to the outside of their respective buildings such as at Sizergh and Levens. The castle was built in the twelfth century but the tower was much later, perhaps after damage was inflicted on the castle in 1460 by the Lancastrian forces. The pele is lived in by the owners of the farm, is private and has no public access. On the south-west side of the castle is Holy Trinity Church of Norman origin.

A major deposit of rich haematite ore was discovered in 1856 at Hodbarrow below the eastern end of what is now the outer barrier. The extracted ore was initially taken to Borwick Rails wharf (top left) a mile away for shipment by boat, but after 1860 more was taken by rail from the station at the newly built town of Millom. It was not until 1868 that the true extent of the ore mass became apparent. It also became apparent that most of this lay either close to the shore or under the sea. This required the development of special techniques to extract it from notoriously dangerous beds of sand and gravel and to guard against incursions of seawater, which were indeed frequent during the whole life of the mine. This protection was provided in the form of barriers, the landward side of which was kept drained by pumps and sluices. The first was a timber barrier built in 1885 nothing of which survives. It was succeeded in 1890 by the more substantial Inner Barrier.

This is the Inner Barrier, completed in 1890, which eventually collapsed due to subsidence, leaving only the end section shown in the photograph. Pumping was done by two massive Cornish beam engines each of 70 inches bore and 10ft stroke, which together with their boilers stood on the open space at the far end of the barrier. They were scrapped when the mine closed in 1968 and the ground was levelled. No trace was left of these formidable engines, capable of lifting water, sand and gravel from 60 fathoms and below and enabling this difficult mine to be worked in reasonable safety. They were superb examples of Victorian engineering and with a little foresight could have formed a working museum of one of the most remarkable places and periods of mining history.

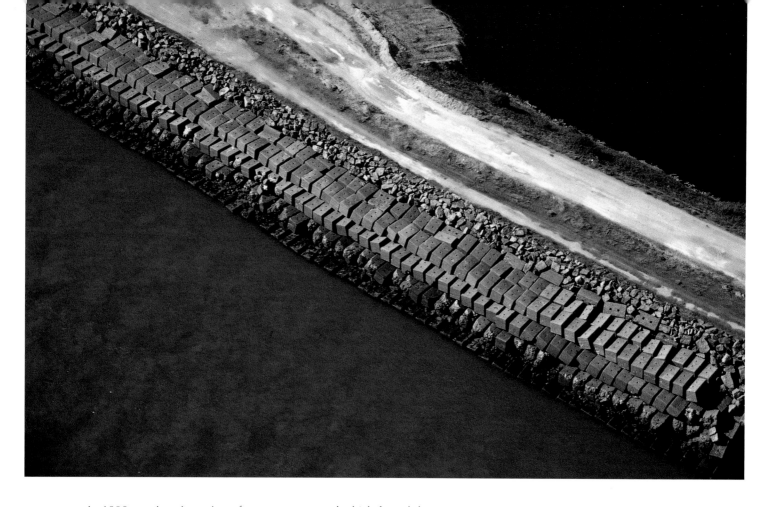

In 1898 a serious incursion of seawater occurred which forced the mining company to plan another, the Outer Barrier, further offshore. It is a mile and a quarter long, was started in 1900 and took a work force of 1200 men five years to complete. The structure consists of separate banks of clay, slag and limestone, faced with concrete blocks on the seaward side. The picture shows the blocks, each weighing 25 tons, carefully laid to break the force of the waves. The Cumbria Coastal Way runs along the top of the barrier where there is a hide for the public to watch the birds on the lagoon. After mining ceased in 1968 and the pumps (by then electric powered) were switched off, the area contained within the barrier quickly flooded. In the words of the Millom poet Norman Nicholson in his poem 'Hodbarrow flooded':

> *The sixty, seventy,*
> *Ninety fathom levels*
> *Are long pipes and throttles of unflowing water,*
> *Stifled cavities,*
> *Lungs of a drowned man.*

The town of Millom did not exist until the Furness Railway came to the old village of Holborn Hill in 1850. In the 1860s ore was being exported more by rail than by ship and at that point Millom came into existence to house and provide for the mine labour force. This is modern Millom and its railway station. It has struggled to survive after the closure of the mine and steel works in 1968.

Haverigg is a quiet village between the northern end of the Outer Barrier and the dunes, on the edge of which is Millom airfield where RAF crews trained in the war. It is now the site of wind turbines and a museum devoted to the history of the airfield. The dunes are the northern part of the lime rich sands noted already at Sandscale and North Walney, with good dune flora.

This is Haverigg looking back the way we have come. In the distance are the lagoon, Outer Barrier and the Duddon Estuary. In the far distance can be seen Askam, the Furness Peninsula and Morecambe Bay.

Silecroft is a small coastal village north of Haverigg with a golf course, camp sites and a railway station.

When we fly north from Silecroft, the coast abruptly changes from dunes to crumbling boulder clay 'cliffs' deeply eroded and scalloped by wind and weather. The beaches are no longer sand but grey gravel.

83

Some of the deeply eroded boulder clay cliffs are as high as 100ft (30m) and present a weird sight from the air especially when the sun is low. Sheep tracks give an impression that some crazy cartographer has decided to draw his contours on the land instead of on the map.

The next river we come to on our flight is the Esk. On its first tidal bend is the farming hamlet of Hall Waberthwaite where the church of St John the Baptist stands in an idyllic position on the very edge of a tidal tributary of the Esk, with views across the estuary and up to the Lake District fells. Believed to have origins in the twelfth century it has suffered little change since the Reformation. Seventeenth century box pews, the pulpit, and most of the interior have escaped the unsympathetic hand of Victorian 'improvement'. John Betjeman describes it as 'the strangest most remote little church'.

Overlooking the church on the opposite side of the River Esk is Muncaster Castle, first built in the thirteenth century and rebuilt and enlarged in the fourteenth century with the addition of a pele tower. The photograph shows the tidal River Esk in the upper left corner, the extensive buildings which house an owl centre, the nursery gardens and the terrace which provides the visitor with spectacular views and a tranquil stroll among the rhododendrons.

Eskmeals and Drigg together form the largest sand dune system in Cumbria. Both are Sites of Special Scientific Interest but the southern threequarters of Eskmeals is excluded, being occupied by the Ministry of Defence's gunnery range. This is Eskmeals looking south with the River Esk on the left.

Above: Now Ravenglass is best known for its narrow gauge steam railway affectionately referred to as 'L'al ratty' which winds its scenic way from the mainline station up the Esk valley to Boot. The photograph shows one of these little trains leaving the station.

Left: Ravenglass is the site of the Roman fort and harbour of Glannoventa. It was built at the western extremity of the mile forts and watch towers of the Roman coastal defence system. It was also at the end of the road from Kendal via Galava (Ambleside) and Hardknott. Being sheltered behind the sand and shingle spits of Drigg and Eskmeals it was an ideal choice to become the principal Roman harbour in the north-west of England. This is the main street of Ravenglass which leads directly down to the water's edge.

The waters of the River Mite come from Wastwater, claimed to be the cleanest and purest of all the lakes in the Lake District and for that reason is called upon to provide the supply for the nuclear site at Sellafield. Here is the River Mite on the left as it goes under the railway bridge to join the Rivers Esk and Irt.

A late winter afternoon with snow on Black Combe, the railway bridge crossing the River Esk, Eskmeals reserve in the middle distance, Drigg dunes on the extreme right and Ravenglass, centre.

The River Irt flows south beneath us with the marshes and dunes of Drigg Nature Reserve on the right. We are directly overhead the north-west coastal boundary of the Lake District National Park, which includes all the coast that we have flown over since passing Silecroft, but tactfully excludes the Drigg low level nuclear waste dump a mile behind us.

As we leave the estuary, the first sight that greets us is the nuclear heart of Cumbria. The low level radioactive waste dump just beyond the River Irt is screened by a conifer plantation and beyond that is the village of Seascale. Dominating the skyline, as it does from all the western fells is the nuclear processing plant of Sellafield, also known at various times as Calder Hall or Windscale. It began producing weapons grade plutonium in 1947 and built the first commercial nuclear power station and the prototype advanced gas-cooled reactor. In 1957 a major incident occurred when a large quantity of radioactive material was released into the surrounding countryside.

92

We have looked at Leighton Moss in Lancashire, Foulshaw and Meathop Mosses in south Cumbria and we shall see something of the even larger Solway Mosses later. But here, two miles south of Seascale is Hallsenna Moor, a National Nature Reserve and the largest raised bog and heath in West Cumbria. Having never been cut for peat, which is unusual, its undisturbed habitat needs no restoration. The site is cared for by Natural England.

As it is forbidden to overfly Sellafield, we shall go inland a few miles to the attractive village of Gosforth, best known for the remarkable Saxon cross in the churchyard. The unique carvings on it represent a stage of transition when the Scandinavians were abandoning their pagan beliefs in favour of Christianity and symbols of both are shown. Perhaps an early example of hedging one's bets.

Calder Abbey was founded under Cistercian rule from Furness Abbey in 1135, but Scottish raids and poor land prevented it from prospering. The church was completed in the late twelfth century with an aisled nave of five bays. All bays on the north (left) side are visible in the photograph, but those on the south side were demolished. The transepts and crossing still stand although the crossing tower has gone, as has the west range of the cloister. However, the east range of the cloister which was rebuilt in the thirteenth century is relatively intact. Look there for the small roofed section. This was the chapter house which was rib vaulted, one bay of which survives. It is interesting to recollect that all we saw of Cockersand Abbey near the start of our flight was the chapter house, there preserved as a family mausoleum. Calder Abbey was dissolved in 1536 by Henry VIII and no doubt much of the stonework found its way into the adjacent Georgian mansion. What is left however is tranquil and inspiring. Despite it being a scheduled ancient monument in the care of English Heritage, it is unfortunately not accessible to the public, being privately owned.

The second picture of Calder Abbey contrasts the serene and peaceful setting of the monastery with its disturbing and sinister background.

Down a lane from the village of Beckermet is old St Bridget's Church. The churchyard has two pre-Norman cross shafts and the interior is simple and basic. Services are no longer regularly held there but in the new church of St John in the village. The Whitehaven & Cleator Railway, the track of which passes to the east of the church, prospered from the 1860s carrying iron ore, coal and passengers until its closure in the 1960s.

This line of well built houses is situated surprisingly on the shore north of Sellafield.

The stained earth around these buildings gives a clue to what has been going on around Egremont for a hundred or more years. Iron ore has been mined in the area since medieval times but it was only after the development of the railway system in the nineteenth century that it became widespread. Subsidence and the network of old railway tracks in the Egremont and Cleator Moor area when seen from the air are evidence of this. This is Florence Mine which closed in 1968. Much of the pithead structures remain and it is now a working museum where visitors are taken on underground tours.

Egremont Castle overlooks the River Ehen at the south end of the town's main street. It was originally constructed of wood in about 1120 and rebuilt in stone at the end of the century. Much of interest remains in what is now a peaceful urban park. The conical mound or motte is on the right and the tall walls of a later keep overshadow it. The gate tower is on the left, access to which was by drawbridge.

To the north of the town of Egremont is Clints Quarry, a source of limestone for the local iron industry. It closed in the 1930s since when a rich limestone flora has developed. It was purchased by Cumbria Wildlife Trust in 1984 and is a Site of Special Scientific Interest. The spoil tips converge towards the entrance gap cut through the limestone rim of the quarry.

There is a legend that in the seventh century an Irish girl, fleeing from an enforced marriage, landed at St Bees, lived here for a time as a hermit, founded a nunnery and was later canonised as St Bega. The church of St Mary and St Bega seen here beyond St Bees School is the church of the twelfth century Benedictine Priory dissolved in 1539. Despite a helping hand from Victorian restorers it still retains some fine parts of the original building, notably the magnificent west doorway and the chancel with its early lancet windows.

St Bees School and Priory Church are seen here in the foreground. Beyond it is the main railway line from Barrow in Furness to Carlisle.

St Bees Head is the largest nesting seabird colony on the west coast of England. The sandstone cliffs are 330ft (100m) high and provide many ledges for breeding seabirds, notably guillemots, razorbills, kittiwakes and fulmars which can be watched from a viewing platform on the cliff top. The cliffs have been an RSPB reserve since 1977.

View of North Head looking south. The small building perched on the cliff edge is a coast guard lookout.

We are looking from North Head across Saltom Bay to Whitehaven and Workington with the hills of Dumfriesshire on the horizon. The Cumbria Coastal Way follows the cliff edge.

Whitehaven Harbour, looking north to Workington and, in the distance, Criffel on the Dumfriesshire coast. In the foreground is Haig Pit and on the extreme lower left are the remains of Saltom Pit.

Haig Pit was the last in the Whitehaven coalfield to be sunk (between 1914 and 1918) and the last to be closed, in January 1986. Its owners, British Coal, abandoned it to its fate and in the next four years it suffered extensive weather damage and vandalism to the pithead machinery. An application was submitted by British Coal early in 1990 for its demolition. This provoked vigorous opposition and a Trust was formed a few months later to preserve and restore the site with its huge Beaver-Dorling winding engines, one of which has been restored to working order. Haig Pit is now one of the foremost mining museums in the north of England.

Saltom Pit is on the shore immediately below Haig Pit. The main shaft was sunk in 1731, eventually reaching a depth of 456 ft (140m) and drained by a large Newcomen pumping engine. The coals were raised by horse ginns and then taken in horse drawn wagons to the staithes (elevated coal stores) in the harbour. It was the first coal mine in England where all its workings were beneath the seabed and what you see in the picture are the remains of the oldest pithead complex in Britain. It was plagued throughout its life, as were all the pits in the Whitehaven coalfield, by methane (fire-damp) where frequent explosions caused great loss of life. Such setbacks encouraged research into ventilation and safe lighting to the benefit of mines and miners everywhere.

Whitehaven had reached the peak of its prosperity by the middle of the nineteenth century, exporting coal and iron ore, importing tobacco and building ships. A slow decline in its fortunes then set in and lasted to the end of coalmining in 1986. This photograph shows the harbour in 1993. The railway lines, no longer needed to take coals to the colliers, have been lifted, but there are remnants of the old commercial activity still evident; fishing boats in South Harbour moored alongside Lime Tongue and Sugar Tongue and merchant ships alongside the wharves in Queen's Dock (top left).

In 1997, the Millennium Commission made a £6M grant for the regeneration of the harbour area. A lock was constructed between the Old Quay and the Old North Wall creating ten hectares of permanent waterspace unaffected by tides. The development of a 100 boat marina in South Harbour and various decorations followed. This photograph shows the completed scheme in 2002. South Harbour has been converted exclusively to leisure activities but commercial ships still have the use of North Harbour and Queen's Dock.

In July 2002 the tall ships visited Whitehaven and two of them are seen here benefiting from the improved facilities. They are moored alongside Sugar Tongue in South Harbour.

West Pier and its lighthouse, immediately beneath us, were constructed between 1824 and 1839 by Sir John Rennie whose father built the Lune Aqueduct which we saw earlier in our flight. The 'Old New Quay' is the small one next and beyond it is Old Quay built progressively between 1634 and 1687, now with the new lock incorporated into its modified end.

The 'monument' in the centre of the photograph known as the 'Candlestick' ventilated Wellington Pit which was opened in 1840. The pithead works covered the whole promontory in the foreground before its closure in 1955. The dark cut across the green field beyond the Candlestick is the Howgill Incline down which loaded coal wagons from Haig Pit were lowered to the harbour. The circular building with the conical roof at the left hand end of the Incline is the Beacon Visitor Centre and Museum.

Five years on and the marina has filled with boats. Even Queen's Dock now accommodates some of the larger leisure boats and the few commercial fishing vessels still using Whitehaven are now out in North Harbour. Note the deep cut of the Howgill Incline running from near the Candlestick down to the Beacon on the harbour.

Right: Restoration of opencast sites is carried out carefully and to a previously agreed plan. This is Keekle in 2004 looking north towards Workington. The track of the old railway line can be seen in the distance and Keekle River has been restored to its original course. But the topographical features which recorded man's activities over many centuries have gone.

Opposite: From Whitehaven to Maryport there is scarcely any open country which has not suffered from opencast coal mining. This photograph is of Keekle on the eastern outskirts of Whitehaven and was taken in 1990. The track of the Cleator and Workington Junction Railway which was closed in 1964 has been buried beneath the topsoil but can be seen in the distance curving round towards Cleator Moor. The River Keekle is temporarily in a culvert.

The green slopes of the hill in the lower right corner of the photograph are the site of the Lowca Foundry, one of the most important engineering works on the Cumbria coast from its start in the late eighteenth century to its closure in 1921. In the middle distance is the village of Parton, the site of an ironworks. Round the furthest promontory is the site of William Pit and Whitehaven is beyond that. The famously scenic railway line to Carlisle closely follows the coast.

In the eighteenth century Harrington exported coal and limestone, had a flourishing shipbuilding industry and later an ironworks which occupied the open space in the lower right of the photograph. But more remarkable is its recent history when, during the last war, it made a major contribution to the war effort. A large industrial complex was constructed in great secrecy close to the ironworks, to extract magnesite from seawater for use in aircraft construction and incendiary bombs. Seawater was pumped from a pumping house on the pier into huge settling tanks on what is now open ground on the right of the photograph. The partly processed solution was then taken away by rail for final processing in the midlands. It was closed in 1953 and Harrington with the benefit of a regeneration grant started its transformation from industry to leisure.

This is Workington looking north towards Maryport. Below us is the mouth of the River Derwent and the entrance to the docks. The long peninsula is not a natural topographical feature but a slag tip from the steel works eroded into black cliffs by wave action. Beyond the nearest group of wind turbines can be seen Siddick Pond which came into existence in the 1870s when the embankment of the new railway prevented the marshes from draining. It is now a nature reserve of reed beds.

Workington Hall was a fine manor house owned by the Curwen family who were responsible for much of the development of Workington's coal industry. It was built in the fourteenth century around a pele tower which can be seen inside the far right corner of the Hall.

Maryport was founded by Humphrey Senhouse in 1748 to export coal brought by wagonway from Broughton Moor down to the mouth of the River Ellen. By the middle of the nineteenth century coal production in the area had increased to such an extent that modern docks were needed to handle it. The first to be constructed was Elizabeth Dock in 1857 (right) and Senhouse Dock (left) in 1884.

Shipbuilding in Maryport was also an important industry from the eighteenth to the twentieth centuries, the yards being on the River Ellen (centre) into which the ships were launched broadside. But coal exports and shipbuilding declined and Maryport like Whitehaven and Harrington turned to the tourist industry for its livelihood. Senhouse Dock is now a marina.

Although Hadrian's Wall ended at Bowness-on-Solway, mile fortlets continued along the coast at least as far as Workington. Seen here is milefortlet 21 situated on a cliff top beside the Maryport to Allonby road near Crosscanonby. Below the cliff are the remains of the Crosscanonby salt pans which were in production from about 1630 to about 1760. The workers' cottages survived for a while but were demolished in the 1970s after which only the circular kinch or evaporating tank, seen here, remains.

Allonby was a Georgian seaside resort and spa with some fine buildings such as the Library, designed by the young Alfred Waterhouse who later went on to design the Natural History Museum in London. Christ Church, in the foreground, was built in 1845.

Another fine building in this attractive seaside village is the listed Grade II public baths opened in 1835. It is seen here in 'The Square' (centre right) with its classical portico.

South of Silloth and a mile inland are the remains of Wolsty Castle, a pele tower built by the monks of Holme Cultram Abbey, it is said, as a safe store for their books, charters and valuables. It is reminiscent of Piel Castle which no doubt served a similar function for the monks of Furness Abbey. Camden in his *Britannia* says the walls of Wolsty were 12ft thick and it was surrounded by a ditch. It is on private land and is not accessible on foot so viewing it from the air is the only way to see it.

Silloth was laid out and planned as an attractive seaside resort to cater for visitors coming from Carlisle on the new Carlisle & Silloth Bay Railway, completed in 1857. The docks were completed in 1859 and a pier was constructed to enable passengers to use the Liverpool, Isle of Man and Whitehaven steamers. It was demolished during the last war. The docks are still very active mainly importing and exporting agricultural goods and the grain for Carr's Mill, seen here. The railway was dismantled in 1964, as were many rural lines everywhere. The remains of the track bed can be seen in the photograph passing beneath the road bridge on its way to the far end of the docks.

Silloth town is fronted by a large open green space with Christ Church in the foreground made from Irish granite. During the last war there was a large RAF base two miles to the east.

Two miles north of Silloth is the village of Skinburness, once a harbour used by the monks of Holme Cultram Abbey, now a small holiday resort.

Above: We are looking across Moricambe Bay towards the Solway Firth in the distance. In the middle distance on the left are the radio masts of Anthorn, a former Royal Naval Air Station, now a NATO signals station used for communicating with submarines. Also at Anthorn are the National Physical Laboratory's atomic clocks where the UK's national time signals originate.

Right: From Skinburness a sand and shingle spit runs out north-east to Grune Point, sheltering Moricambe Bay and Skinburness Marsh to the east, well known and visited for its flora and birds, especially during the migrations.

Holme Cultram Abbey was founded in 1150 on the southern edge of Moricambe Bay on marshy ground which the Cistercian monks diligently set about draining and cultivating. It has had a troubled history, being in the border area affected by the wars between Edward I and the Scots. It suffered neglect after its dissolution in 1536 like most monastic establishments and in 1600 the tower collapsed. During the course of repair the roof was accidentally set on fire by a workman using a live coal as a light to look for a chisel. In 1703 the size of the church was reduced to its present ground plan. But the worst misfortune of all occurred on the 9th of June 2006 when in an act of vandalism worse than any since the Dissolution the Abbey was set on fire and almost completely destroyed.

Within a month, the debris from the fire had been removed.

By February 2008 restoration had been started.

Wedholme Flow lies a short distance to the east of Holme Cultram Abbey and is the only raised bog on the Solway Mosses National Nature Reserve still being actively cut for peat. According to Natural England these mosses are 10,000 years old and reach a depth of 14 metres, much of which has already gone to garden centres for growbags and potted plants. Natural England have started the restoration of these unique habitats by buying out some of the peat extraction companies' rights but as my photograph shows, the damage is serious, widespread and will be long lasting. In the distance to the right is Moricambe Bay and beyond it Criffel and the coast of Dumfriesshire.

The Solway Junction Railway opened in September 1869. It was a branch of the Carlisle & Silloth Bay Railway which crossed Glasson Moss from Kirkbride to this embankment on the Solway coast. A viaduct, 1940 yards (1773m) long, carried the line from here over the Solway to Seafield on the coast of Dumfriesshire. It was built by James Brunlees the engineer who also built the Kent and Leven Viaducts which we saw earlier in our flight. In the winter of 1881 it was severely damaged by ice floes 'up to 10ft thick' coming down the Solway on an ebb tide. It carried freight and passengers until its closure in 1921 and it was demolished in 1933. It is said that on Sundays, Scots on the north side would frequently walk across it to take advantage of English licensing laws. Glasson Moss is a National Nature Reserve and is considered to be the best and largest example of a lowland raised mire in England.

A mile to the east of the railway embankment lies the village of Bowness-on-Solway whose coastal strip is owned by the National Trust and which is within the Solway Coast Area of Outstanding Natural Beauty. In Roman times it was the site of Maia, the western most fort of Hadrian's wall, little of which remains to-day, although it is said that there are Roman foundations beneath St Michael's Church (middleground left). In the middle ages there was a low tide crossing here where guides led people across the estuary.

Port Carlisle, two miles east of Bowness-on-Solway, was built for the Carlisle Canal which opened in 1823. This was just over 11 miles in length and had eight locks enabling small ships to reach the centre of Carlisle. In 1853 it closed and in the following year the canal bed was converted to a railway. It carried freight and also, after 1899, passengers in small horse drawn carriages called 'Dandy cars', one of which is preserved in York Railway Museum. These continued working until 1914 when the line became steam hauled. In the photograph can be seen the remains of the lock (upper right). The bed of the canal can then be traced passing beneath a bridge and curving round amongst the trees to pass in front of the village.

This photograph shows the remains of the harbour wall which provided shelter for the lock entrance.

The Carlisle & Silloth Bay Railway crossed Drumburgh Moss before joining the Port Carlisle Railway for its last few miles into Carlisle. Drumburgh Moss is a National Nature Reserve managed by Cumbria Wildlife Trust and is a fine example of a raised mire. The photograph shows the old railway track across the Moss and Port Carlisle in the extreme upper left.

Burgh Marsh is where Edward I died on his return to Holme Cultram Abbey and a monument marks the spot. Of great importance for wildfowl and once heavily shot over by punt gunners, Burgh Marsh stretches to Rockcliffe Marsh (in the distance, left). In the extreme lower right of the photograph can be seen the route of the Carlisle Canal, which was subsequently turned into the track of the Port Carlisle Railway, the course of the Roman vallum and the modern road.

The A74 trunk road and the main west coast railway line to Scotland here cross the River Esk. Beyond that is Rockcliffe Marsh with the River Eden beyond it on the far left. The marshes of the Upper Solway Firth form one of the largest areas of intertidal habitat in Britain, equal in size to Morecambe Bay or the Wash and are of international importance for wading birds and migrating and breeding wildfowl. In the far distance can be seen Moricambe Bay, another important roosting site for geese.

Left: Carlisle Castle was built by William Rufus in 1092 so ensuring that Carlisle was in English hands for most of its subsequent history. The oldest part is the square twelfth century keep in the farthest corner of the inner bailey, the entrance to which is over the half moon battery. In the centre of the photograph can be seen Carlisle Cathedral.

Opposite: Carlisle Cathedral has a strange history. It was founded in 1122 as an Augustinian priory and built with a nave of eight bays and a chancel of two. Later, the chancel was extended to eight making it of equal length to the nave. However, during the Civil War in the seventeenth century, the parliamentary forces demolished six bays of the nave, leaving its shape the exact reverse of the original. It is a wonderful cathedral, full of beauty and interest, not least the east window, chancel ceiling and carvings of the misericords. The photograph shows the monks' refectory (lower centre).

142

Having started our flight by looking at the tallest structure on the coast of north-west Lancashire, it seems appropriate to finish by looking at a building with the tallest structure in Carlisle. Here is the Shaddon Mill built by Peter Dixon and Sons in 1836 for spinning cotton, then a major industry in the city. Later, it changed to woollen power-loom weaving. The power had been provided from the beginning by steam engines whose boilers were sited beneath this massive chimney. Dixon's chimney when built was 305ft (93m) high, then the tallest mill chimney in Europe but now reduced to 275ft (84m). Thankfully both it and the magnificent Victorian mill building itself with its seven storeys and 351 windows are Grade II listed structures. Now it has been converted to apartments, but that must surely be a better option than demolition.